A Smart Guide to Building Wealth: Money Moves Your Parents Wish They Had Made

Ann Otten

Copyright © 2021 by Ann Otten

All rights reserved. Any unauthorized reprint or use of this material is prohibited. No part of this book may be reproduced or transmitted in any form or by any means, electronic or mechanical, including photocopying, recording, or by any information storage and retrieval system without express written permission of the copyright owner except for the use of quotations in a book review.

Disclaimer: While all attempts have been made to verify the accuracy of the information provided in this publication, the author assumes no responsibility for any errors or omissions. The author will not be held responsible for any repercussions beyond the scope of this book.

Thank you to my parents and financial advisors for putting me in a position to be able to share my wealth of knowledge and to empower others to do the same. Most of all, thank you to God, to whom all great blessings flow.

e you can invest your money so that you can build a
rous life. These ideas are based on my personal
rom continuous research and aid from professional
nners with many years of experience.

irst, in order to build any wealth, you will need to
king account. This can be done at any local bank and
a minimum amount required in the account—
maller amount, like $500. A checking account is
cause you don't have to keep track of your cash.
ctly deposit money from your job into it, and you
money from the checking account using a debit card

research and check out different checking (and
ns that different banks have. Each bank can vary
es to monthly maintenance fees, minimum balances,
n account charges. Keep location and convenience
n choosing a bank if you are going to make frequent
ns for visiting could include depositing or
; cash from your accounts or depositing checks. The
lets me deposit checks through their mobile app,
es the visits to a bank location. That's a huge
or me.

Table of Contents

Chapter 1: Work Smarter, Not Harder 1

Chapter 2: Rich Mentality 4

Chapter 3: Different Paths to Wealth 7

Chapter 4: Create a Budget and Make Goals 11

Chapter 5: Good Debt Versus Bad Debt 18

Chapter 6: Housing 36

Chapter 7: Investments 45

Chapter 8: Other Ways to Save 53

Chapter 9: Ready, Set, Go! 59

Chapte
Work Smarter,

The point of this book is to have you
harder. There are things that I wish I
could have helped me as I lived on n
responsibility for my own money. Fo
that I should have started saving as e
money can grow exponentially over

Simple tricks and a foundation of kn
future full of financial prosperity. Yo
making an hourly wage, but you will
you are at your job. How can you get
earn more than the hours you physica
putting your money where it can wor

Later in this book, I will get into inve
to start growing your wealth. Investin
putting your money in different place
Investing is a way to make passive in
when you earn money without having
(Sounds pretty good to me!) In this bc

options whe
more prosp
experience
financial pl

First things
open a chec
usually has
typically a
beneficial b
You can di
can retrieve
or check.

Feel free to
savings) pl
when it cor
or overdra
in mind wh
visits. Reas
withdrawir
bank I have
which redu
advantage

A Smart Guide to Building Wealth:
Money Moves Your Parents Wish They Had Made

You also have the option to open a savings account. A savings account should be used a bit differently. A savings account is just that—money sitting in an account that is used as savings. It should be considered "untouchable" and used more as an emergency fund. A good starting point is to have three to six months' worth of expenses saved up for when something out of your control happens. This could be placed in your savings account for when your car breaks down or if you lose your job for a short time. You can always transfer money from your savings into your checking account, but otherwise, you are not able to access it through your debit card.

Some people never get beyond this point because they spend the money they have in those accounts. They are never able to build up enough money to have extra to spend. That's why budgeting is crucial. If you build up a lot of money in your savings account, some will advise that a typical savings account is no longer needed if you can access the money elsewhere. You can invest this money into other areas, which we will get to later, that could serve the same purpose and earn you more money in the long run.

Chapter 2: Rich Mentality

The mentality of being a saver rather than a spender is a big hurdle to overcome but can be a big step to becoming wealthy. Millionaires and billionaires only *stay* that way if they know how to manage their money. It's very easy to lose it all. People who win the lottery are great examples of this. Research shows that many lottery winners will lose all of their winnings within a couple of years and are left worse off than before they won. The simple concept still stands—you can't spend more money than you have coming in.

What is important to you in this life? Is it going on beautiful vacations? Is it having a family one day? Being able to retire? Owning a home? All of the above? Then you must begin to work towards those goals now and put plans in place to achieve them. You need to pick and choose things that are worth your time and money, and you may even have to make small sacrifices at times to keep to your goals. For some, this is the biggest battle.

A Smart Guide to Building Wealth:
Money Moves Your Parents Wish They Had Made

With social media, it might seem like you always need to keep up with the latest gadgets and material things to be cool and fit in. However, there is not enough money to buy it all, nor would you want to. So, you have to keep your priorities and your long-term goals in mind.

There will always be someone who is richer and who has more than you. That's a fact of life. Just remember, the grass is greener where you water it. You should remember that social media is a highlight reel. You see someone who bought a brand-new car, but what you don't see behind the screen is that they can't afford that car and that they are in debt. Comparison is the thief of joy. So, go after your goals and what will ultimately make *you* happy, and you can rest easy with your decisions.

One of the most important reasons to have a saving mentality is to keep you out of trouble and set you up for success. You may be reading this as a young person and think what you do now doesn't matter, but it does. What you do now has a huge impact on your future. If you decide to go to college and go into $200,000 in debt, that will have a huge impact on your financial future. You may be paying that debt back until the day you die. You must start thinking about your goals now and how you want your future to look.

When you think about your financial future and how you want to earn more and buy more things, you must put something into perspective. If you earn $1,000 more and you spend $1,000 more than before, you are left with zero. You have not increased your wealth. In order to really grow your money, you either need to spend less or earn more to make sure you aren't netting out at zero as your wealth builds. For example, if you get a big promotion at work, you can treat yourself, but ultimately, you should try to live as you were prior to the promotion in order to put the additional cash you earn to work.

Chapter 3: Different Paths to Wealth

Wealth can take place in a multitude of ways. The trick to finding the right path to wealth is doing the next right thing for you and your goals. My husband and I have somewhat similar paths, but that doesn't have to be your case. There can be setbacks, like losing a job that you don't expect or having to buy a different car because your old used car finally died. It's about continuing to move forward, not spending money you don't have, and working on the next step to your goal.

You may have short dips in the overall trajectory, but overall, your financial path should continue moving upward. Hopefully, as you learn common pitfalls to avoid, you can grow your wealth quicker as you go. As you'll notice in the examples below, each person has focused on paying down debt sooner rather than later, which will be key to you as you start to grow your wealth.

My Path:
- Checking, savings account
- College: student credit card, four years of private college with soccer scholarship
- After college: full-time job with benefits, 401(k), moved in with my brother for a cheap rent, paid off student loans and car payment, Roth IRA, health savings account, bought townhome, sold townhome, got married (joint bank account) and bought first home

Husband's Path:
- Checking, savings account
- College: part-time job, state college for five years, credit card
- After college: full-time job with benefits, 401(k), lived at home with parents to pay off school debt and car payment, saved up for a down payment, bought townhome, got married (joint bank account), sold townhome, bought first home

Friend's Path:
- Checking, savings account
- College: two years of trade school

- After college: credit card, full-time job with benefits, 401(k), rent apartment, paid off student loans, bought home, paid off car

There will also be people you meet in life who have very different scenarios from the outside looking in. That is the key in the following scenario here. These two people in the next example are very different, but one is truly rich because they are not stressed about money and are able to feel content and happy.

Person 1: electrician, $75,000 salary, paid off student loans, no car payment, no credit card debt, almost paid off home, married and happy, not stressed about money

Person 2: real estate agent, $1.2 million salary, owes $1 million in credit card debt, student loans, car loans, and mortgages, travels to second home on the beach, single, goes out to eat every night, always wanting more things to keep up with society, always stressed about money

The things you don't see on the outside of these two people are what's important. You will never know someone else's situation and how they can afford things. The funny thing is they may not be able to afford their belongings because they are spending money they don't have.

Not having to worry about money can set you up to be truly content. Wealth does not mean you have to make a million-dollar salary. By building your money through savings and investments, you can get the wealth you want without the hassle of bad debt and stress.

Chapter 4:
Create a Budget and Make Goals

One trick to managing money that is often overlooked because it seems so basic, is establishing a budget. How do you *really* know how much you are earning and spending without tracking it? You don't. You're just guessing. If you're guessing, you can't use your money in the most profitable way.

Budgeting can seem scary and annoying if you approach it with the attitude that it is going to make you restrict your expenditures. It doesn't have to be looked at in a negative light. Budgeting is simply a fancy way to say you are tracking your money to see where it goes. It doesn't necessarily mean you are depriving yourself or restricting your spending.

There are many ways to do a budget, but the simplest form that has worked for me is in a simple Excel spreadsheet. By using a spreadsheet, you can lay out all your earnings and expenses. It's also a very good way to track your overall wealth, including assets and liabilities. Again, assets are anything that has value. For example, if you own a car, it is an asset and has value whether it's completely paid for or not. A bank sees it as something of value that you could potentially use as collateral if you were strapped for cash. In the case of budgeting, just to keep things simple, we aren't talking about furniture or other small possessions you have.

Liabilities are the opposite of assets and include debt or anything that reduces your overall wealth. A car can be both an asset and a liability. For example, if you bought a used car for $10,000, paid off $6,000, and still have $4,000 principle remaining to be paid, the asset is now $6,000 (less any depreciation) and the liability is $4,000.

Here is a simple example of what a budget could look like. At the end of each month, all you need to do is enter all your earnings and expenses from the previous month. You may only have a checking and savings account, but eventually, you could have info coming from credit cards, Roth IRA, and other streams of money to enter. So for now, this is a good place to begin. Double check everything you are entering, including free-flowing cash that can come from birthday money or babysitting. Entering this all into one document provides an exact snapshot of exactly where your money is in order to make decisions. Over time, you can continue to add more and more details to your budget so it can look more advanced, depending on what detail you want to see.

	Jan	Feb	Mar
Income	$1,500	$1,700	$1,500
Expenses	$800	$850	$1,550
Monthly Total	+$1,200	+$1,650	($50)
Account Totals			
Checking Account	$1,200	$2,850	$2,800
Savings Account	$3,000	$3,000	$3,000

One way to add depth to your budget is to start placing your expenses into categories. This allows you to see which areas are taking up most of your spending. Generally speaking, a good rule of thumb to remember is the "50/30/20 Rule", a rule which financial professional Dave Ramsey often talks about. Allocate 50% of your income to your fixed expenses and essentials, like housing, insurance, car payments, school loan payments and food. Wants take care of 30% and include things that are not necessary, but things you want to do, like movies, sporting events, and eating at restaurants. Savings should be allocated to 20% of your overall budget. This is a quick way to gauge your monthly numbers and see if you are overspending in any of your categories. If your wants are the majority of your spending, it may be time to cut back and focus on putting money towards your debt. Luckily, wants should be the easiest expenditures to cut back on, as they are not essentials or necessities.

	Category	Jan	Feb	Mar
Income	Part Time Job	$1,500.00	$1,500.00	$1,500.00
	Birthday Gift	$ -	$ 200.00	$ -
	Total Income	$1,500.00	$1,700.00	$1,500.00
Expenses	Car (loan, insurance, gas)	$650.00	$650.00	$700.00
	Phone	$50.00	$50.00	$50.00
	Food	$100.00	$ 50.00	$ 150.00
	Entertainment	$ -	$100.00	$650.00
	Total Expenses	$800.00	$850.00	$1,550.00
Monthly Total		+$700.00	+$850.00	($50.00)
Account Totals				
Checking Account		$700.00	$1,550.00	$1,500.00
Savings Account		$3,000.00	$3,000.00	$3,000.00

Okay, so you've entered your numbers into the budget. Now is where the goals come in to keep your eyes on the prize and put your budget to use. Where do you want your money to be in one year, five years, or ten years? You don't have to have an exact number as an answer, but you should always be working towards those goals. Year over year, you are probably wanting your money to continue to grow. Some examples of small goals could be slowly trying to eliminate your debt, start saving for a trip, or getting a part-time job to save more. The best way is to start small and work from there.

As a young person, the biggest key to savings and helping your money grow is to remember that compounding interest is on your side. Compounding interest is equivalent to the snowball effect. One small snowflake can roll and roll into a large snowball. Just think, if you collect change everywhere and you put those pennies, nickels, dimes, and quarters into a jar, after a year later, you look at the full jar and realize you've actually collected a couple hundred dollars.

The point is, small amounts can seriously add up. Compounding interest is similar. If you invest money into an account that pays you 5% annual interest, you can see in the following chart how quickly it can grow without touching it. The more you put in, the more it can grow over time. This is the key to investing. How can we get your money to grow on its own without having to do anything? This is the stuff that is exciting! Free money? Sign me up! As you can see, the longer you can keep your money in, the more it grows. As a young person, it's important to start investing early and often, so it can do the work for you!

Compounding 5% Interest Over 20 Years

Initial Investment	$100	$1,000	$10,000
Year 1	$105	$1,050	$10,500
Year 2	$110.25	$1,102.50	$11,025
Year 5	$127.63	$1,276.28	$12,762.82
Year 10	$162.89	$1,628.89	$16,288.95
Year 20	$265.33	$2,653.30	$26,532.98

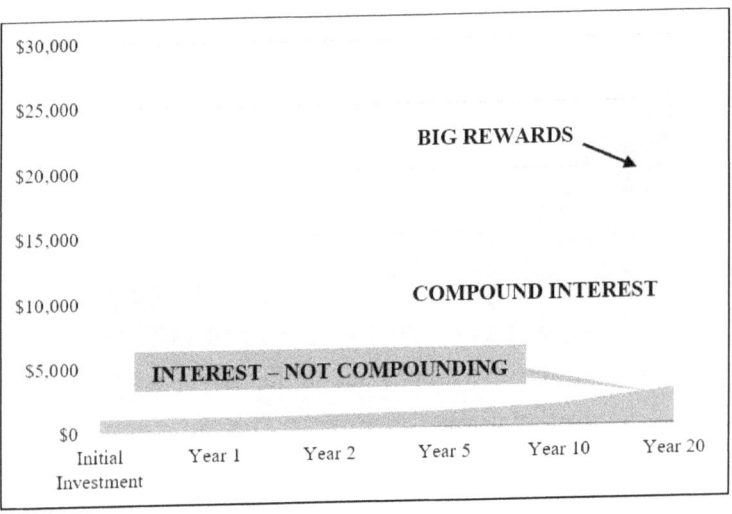

Once you have created a budget and are starting to save some money, it doesn't mean you can never go out to eat or buy new clothes, but it does mean you need to be conscious of how you are spending your money. Now that you are tracking your money, you know how much you can spend within reason.

Being a saver is one of those things that you might mentally have to remind yourself over and over. There are times when I have a lot of activities and purchases going on, but I make sure to also have times when I try to reduce my spending and save money. So, if you go on a small shopping spree during the holidays, it's not the end of the world. It's just a conscious decision, and maybe the following months, you have to reduce your spending. It's all about balance and focusing on your long-term goals.

It's also important to note that there is not just one way to get rich. Everyone's goals and passions are different. For one person, retiring early is important. For another, it is traveling and going out to eat, and for someone else, it is buying a home one day. However, with every decision, there is a sacrifice. If your goal is to own a home, you may have to sacrifice and save a significant amount for a down payment. If your goal is to travel, you may not be able to own a home. This is why you have goals in place. You now have something to reference and keep in mind when you are deciding whether to make a purchase or not.

Chapter 5: Good Debt Versus Bad Debt

Going into debt is the quickest way to get into trouble and potentially ruin your future. Debt should be taken seriously because some people are never able to dig themselves out of the hole. In this book, we want to talk about how to invest your money, but if you are constantly paying off debt, then you probably won't be doing any investing. Your money will be better spent paying off your debts. So again, take debt very seriously.

Debt also plays a huge part in your credit. A credit score is a number that tells the banks how good you are at paying off bills and loans. They use it to determine how risky it is to loan you money. A credit score ranges from 300-850 points and is based on your payment history, length of credit history, and ability to pay on time. Missed or late payments, as well as a short history of credit, could result in a low credit score. The higher your credit score, the better. If you have a low credit score or a lot of debt, you might not be able to get a new loan or purchase a home, as banks won't trust you to be smart with their money.

This is why a large amount of student loan debt can become a factor in your financial future if it's not dealt with.

In order to start building a credit score, you can become an authorized user on a parent's credit card, or you could get one of your own. The key is to make sure you are always paying off the monthly balance on time. Essentially, if you don't have the money sitting in your checking or savings account to pay for something, you shouldn't buy it.

Cash on hand is considered a liquid asset. Liquidity is how liquid or easy it is to get to your cash. A checking account is liquid and you can access it immediately, whereas a retirement account is not because it has restrictions on when and how you can get to that money. It might be locked down for you to access for some time.

The main point to remember with debt is to pay it off as quickly as you can. The interest won't be able to build up, and you can have the stress of it off your plate. Not to mention, you can start saving your money and investing. If you have bad debt, you should not be worried about investing because that debt will continue to grow and hurt your overall wealth. Your main goal should be to eliminate that debt completely.

Credit cards can be very useful tools. The best reason to use a credit card is to start building your credit. Landlords and employers are good examples of people who can investigate your credit history. It is better not to have anything on there that might deter them from trusting you, so it's important to be responsible with your money. Without having credit, others might not be willing to take a risk on whether you will be dependable or not. So, it's important to start small and to be responsible.

Each month after you pay your full credit card payment, you are showing banks that you are reliable. In turn, this will help increase your credit score. It doesn't have to be a ton of money each month. It can just be a few purchases. You are still showing the banks that you are dependable and capable of paying off your debt.

One of the easiest ways to get into debt is with credit cards. They can be fun and rewarding, which is why they are so enticing, but there is also a dark side to them. If you carry over a credit card balance rather than paying it off every month, you will be charged extra interest. This can add up quickly over time and can result in racking up thousands of dollars in credit card debt.

The key to a credit card is using it similar to a debit card. Each month, only buy things that you have cash in your checking account to pay off. Set yourself a calendar reminder. Then at the end of each month, pay your credit card bill so you are not charged with any extra fee. If you do not carry over a balance to the next month, you will not be charged extra from the credit card company. This is how you build a good credit history and will help increase your credit score over time.

When choosing a credit card, you want to be careful with the annual fee (APR or Annual Percentage Rate). The one I use often for all my purchases builds up enough rewards throughout the year to offset the $99 annual fee. However, you also have the option to call your credit card company and ask them to waive your annual fee. If you are in good financial standing with your credit card company, they may waive the annual fee, which is an easy way to save money.

Typically, if you are just getting started, I would suggest getting a credit card without an annual fee as a simple way to slowly build credit without any extra expenses. If you do a little research, there are sites that compare the best credit cards for your criteria. Find a credit card that gives you a low interest rate and the right rewards for you to get the most out of your purchases.

The best part about credit cards are the rewards! They can provide you with cash back for every purchase or even give you traveling miles as a bonus reward. For that reason, I like to use every purchase from gas to groceries on my credit card rather than my debit card. I want to earn as many rewards as I can from my purchases. Again, I am only purchasing what I have money in my bank account to pay for. I personally like to save up my rewards for a trip or something that would be expensive and have those rewards help pay for it. That way, you don't see a huge spike in your overall expenditures at the end of the month. Another great way to use those rewards is to help pay off your monthly balance.

Student loan debt is another bad type of debt that needs to get paid off as soon as possible. Education can be a great investment in your future and potential career. However, when it comes to education, student loans are becoming larger and tougher to pay back if you decide to go to college. If you get into too much debt, you may be paying it off your entire life, which greatly affects your financial future.

A Smart Guide to Building Wealth:
Money Moves Your Parents Wish They Had Made

Student loans can be such a big expense that you may need to do some significant thinking and upfront planning. As a young student, I would have liked to know more about student loans before going into college. Going into debt can profoundly affect your future. There are many ways that you can go about getting an education while still being responsible with your money.

The first item to consider is the end goal or your potential career. If you finish college and start out as an intern or in an introductory position, you know you will make a smaller salary than if you are starting out as a lawyer or doctor. With an introductory salary, you could be looking at $30,000. This is important to note because you will have to start paying back your student debt a year after graduation. So, if you're sitting with $200,000 in debt, you could be in trouble. You can't realistically pay that back in a short amount of time with the salary you have. With the amount of interest on the loan, you may be paying that back until you die or even worse—pass it onto your children.

Below is a calculation of a $200,000 loan with 4% interest displaying how that debt could grow over time. Your monthly payment could be as much as a mortgage! It's important to note that the quicker you can pay off these loans the better. You can always pay down more than the monthly payment. As you can see, the longer it takes you, the more money you end up paying in total due to interest. Get rid of bad debt as soon as you can. Why pay more if you don't have to?

Monthly Payment for $200,000 Student Loan, 4% Interest

Loan Term	Monthly Payment	Total Lifetime Cost (due to interest)
5 Years	$3,683	$220,998
10 Years	$2,025	$242,988
20 Years	$1,212	$290,871
30 Years	$955	$343,739

Source: SmartAsset.com

There are better solutions. One way you can save on a college education is with scholarships. A scholarship provides money off your annual tuition. There are scholarships out there for everything you could think of that will save you money. Most commonly, these could be in sports, academics, or even having an alum as a relative. However, if you spend some time doing research, you will find random ones, such as scholarships for future teachers or even tall people. As crazy as they sound, these could quickly tick off thousands of dollars you might owe, so it's worth a shot to apply for the ones that may be suitable for you.

Another route you could take for college to save money is to go to community college for two years and transfer to a public or private college. Typically, a community college is where you can get your general elective classes out of the way while saving quite a bit of money. The only catch is that you need to find out up front if the community college will transfer your credits to the next college you plan to attend. This is very important if you are trying to save time and money, because you will want to make sure you don't have to start over at the next school, whether it is a state college or a private university. Either way, it's likely that a four-year state or private college will be more expensive than a community college or junior college. Some high schools also allow students to earn college credits while still in high school, which can significantly reduce the amount of time the person would have to spend in college. Being aware and able to take those classes can also be helpful in the long run. In the next table you will see college tuition broken down for four different types of students.

	STUDENT A	STUDENT B	STUDENT C	STUDENT D
	State College	Community College, Transfer to State College	Private College	Program Specific
Year 1	$25,000	$5,000	$50,000	$35,000
Year 2	$25,000	$5,000	$50,000	$35,000
Year 3	$25,000	$25,000	$50,000	$35,000
Year 4	$25,000	$25,000	$50,000	$35,000
Year 5	$25,000			$35,000
Year 6				$35,000
TOTAL	$125,000	$60,000	$200,000	$210,000

Student A is going to a state college, which is a popular route for many students. Public schools are typically less expensive than private schools. With state schools, however, it may take you five years instead of four to finish depending on your program. Student B is going to a community college for the first two years and will transfer to finish their degree—in this case, to a public college. Student C is choosing to attend a prestigious private school, and Student D is going into a pharmacy program that will be six years instead of the typical seven years somewhere else.

In each of these cases, each student chose the best solution for their education, and they can still find some ways to save money. Student A is opting for a public education because the school is a close drive, so they can commute rather than live on campus, which will save that expense. They are in the business program, which their advisor said would typically take five years to finish. If they take a few summer courses at a community college or online, which are usually less expensive, they can try to cut that down to four years. Now they are saving a year of time and expenses and are also able to start earning a full-time salary sooner than expected.

Student B is paying for school on their own, but they want to continue their education. So, they are going to a community college for two years and are working a part-time job on the side to help fund their schooling. After two years, they will transfer to a public school to finish their degree.

Student C is attending a specific program at a private school, but will be getting a partial athletic and academic scholarship. Her parents have also saved up and will be helping her with some of the tuition cost so that she doesn't end up with a huge loan after her four years.

If you know you want to be in a specific profession, like pharmacy for Student D, you may be able to find a school or program that may cut out a full year of extra cost. You are still saving money in that way. Yes, it will still be expensive in the short term, but you will be saving yourself time and money by going into a specific track. Also, going into a field like pharmacy, you know you will be able to pay back those loans after you become a professional and start earning a high starting salary.

Once you earn an undergraduate degree, you may want to further your education and get a master's degree. Instead of jumping into it right away, you may be able to save money, depending on your career. Many companies have programs that will pay for partial or even full tuition if you are an employee. This could be an easy avenue to reduce the overall amount of student loans that could bury you and, at the same time, could provide an income. There may be caveats with these programs as far as how long you may have to stay at the company after you earn your degree or what grade average you need to maintain in a master's program. Each company has its own policies regarding employee education.

Yes, school can be quite a huge expense, but there are ways to cut costs. Hopefully, you can now look at education with a new financial lens to make a better decision regarding your future. Ultimately, it is always wise to invest in yourself because that is how you grow and give yourself more opportunities. However, you don't have to let it break the bank.

Another way to find yourself in trouble with debt is with cars. Unless you've paid cash for your car and have no outstanding payments, a car can be considered a liability or possible bad debt. The unfortunate fact about cars is that they lose their value quickly. When you drive a brand-new car off the lot, it automatically loses value within seconds. Personally, I would never buy a new car for this reason. Typically, you can't sell a new car for as much as you paid for it, and it usually looks and functions the exact same as a slightly used car, without the high price tag. That is why cars are one of those things you should be careful with.

In regard to leasing a car, my advice is to never lease a car because you want your money to be put to better use somewhere else. By leasing a car, you are essentially renting it, and over the long term, you will probably be paying more than if you originally purchased it. The only good option to leasing a car would be if it is a short-term lease. For example, if you are living somewhere for a short stint, it may be worth it to lease rather than make a significant purchase.

You might find that some people enjoy having nice things they normally wouldn't be able to afford. For some, having a brand-new car is very important to them, and in this case, having a lease may be a better option than the purchase. Because a new car can be expensive, having a lease can save you some money in the short-term. However, I would still not recommend it. Usually there are few differences between a slightly used car and a brand new one, so I don't see the financial reasoning in needing a more expensive version simply because it's "new".

If you do decide to lease a car, keep in mind that a typical lease is three years. The downside is that you need a large down payment upfront and then at the end of the lease you may be charged with a bunch of additional fees, depending on your contract. Sometimes you may be charged if you have reached a certain mileage amount, if you have any accident, or if you return the car in less than excellent condition. After the lease is up, you still do not own a car. So again, I would not recommend investing lots of your money into leasing a vehicle. Financially, you may not be better off than when you started, which is the goal with your money decisions.

Cars are expensive, but this is where a savings account comes in so you can save enough money to buy one. Keep in mind, you will also need to pay for car insurance. The more expensive the car, the more expensive your insurance will be. However, there are ways to be creative when you want to save money. When I wanted to purchase a car, I had $15,000 saved up, and my dad helped fund the other $5,000 with his own money. Instead of me owing the dealership the extra $5,000, I now owed my dad. I was able to pay him back the $5,000 slowly without any interest. It worked out much better for me because I was able to own the car rather than lease it. The quicker you can get rid of bad debt, the better.

Cars can be a tricky purchase because of their high value. Going into a car purchase, you want to find out as much as you can to know what the car is worth. You want to be sure you are getting what you pay for. This may be different than the price it is being sold at. There are a couple of things to note that could save you money in the long run. Make sure you research the car you're interested in buying, so you can find out if it has been in any previous accidents or required any major repairs. This can usually be done online with a simple search to find out the car facts. You could also have an independent mechanic take a quick inspection of the car at a relatively low cost before you buy it. Having an expert take a look could potentially save you a lot of money in the long run. They will be able to tell you about possible future problems or if anything is likely to need replacing soon. If there are issues, you'll then be able to negotiate your purchase price or select another car to purchase. If there are no issues with the car you're interested in, you will know you are buying a sound car.

I would also try to avoid purchasing extra add-ons or extended warranties the dealership may try to sell you. Many times, if the car is fairly new, they already have extended warranties on it, and the dealer is persuading you into purchasing more than you need. Or many dealerships already have a limited time warranty on used cars, such as a 90-day or 3,000-mile guarantee for any maintenance problems. Without purchasing extra add-ons or extended warranties, you will be able to cut unneeded costs.

It might seem strange to think about, but marriage is another avenue that can lead to debt and should be a calculated risk when it comes to your wealth. One of the most common reasons for divorce is financial stress, so it is important to figure out the foundation of your financial relationship before it can become detrimental. First off, you want to have open communication in your relationship prior to getting married. That shouldn't stop when it comes to discussing money. Being able to discuss your situations will take honesty and will hopefully bring you closer together. This will also help in your future whenever you face difficult discussions and decisions as a couple.

It is important to understand your future spouse's debt scenario. Are they sitting with credit card debt, a car payment, and student loans? If that is the case, you need to know that now because if you want to buy a home together, you might be denied. You also want to have a plan in place to help them get rid of their debt. Suddenly, you might realize that all your income should go towards your spouse's bad debt instead of your wedding. Yes, paying debt takes priority and sacrifice to get rid of sometimes. I should also point out that a wedding is definitely not worth going into debt over and starting your life together on a stressful note. Remember, you should not be spending money you physically don't have.

When choosing a partner, you want to be on the same page when it comes to financial goals. If you are wanting to save, but they are not on board, you will have a problem. Saving and working towards your financial goals will be a lot quicker and easier if you have the same plan in mind and are working in one direction as a unit. This is also why I would recommend a joint checking and savings account rather than individual accounts.

A joint account is where all of the money is pooled together as a couple. Yes, you can see each other's expenses, and that can sometimes be a small hurdle to get over. However, I would suggest checking in with each other at least once at the end of each month to discuss how you can stay on track with your budgeting and to see how things are going. Eventually, you're likely to realize, if it falls within your overall budget, the small little purchases each person makes won't bother you as much. For the purposes of budgeting and goals, it becomes much easier to increase your wealth as a unit and will ultimately lead to a richer life.

A category of good debt you can have is owning a home or having a mortgage. A mortgage is a payment you have on your home. This is a debt you won't have to pay off immediately. However, in buying a home, you want to avoid going "house broke". That is when your mortgage payment is too high, and you are hardly able to pay for anything else, like food or other essentials. Even if your bank approves you to purchase a million-dollar home, you have to realistically be able to pay each monthly payment.

Other costs come up in owning a home that you might not have initially thought about, like property taxes, utilities, or furniture for your home. Furniture and essentials inside the home will cost money, so just realize it may not be wise to purchase at the top of your budget. You don't have to purchase your dream home right away, and it may take time to get there.

Having a budget in place will help you make a realistic decision on what you will be able to afford. To put it simply, the bank wants as much money as they can get, so it is in their best interest, not necessarily yours, if you purchase a more expensive home.

Chapter 6: Housing

One of the biggest costs to your budget or salary can be the cost of living. As a rule, it should never be more than 30% of your gross monthly income, so you can actually live off of the rest. Since living can be such a large cost, it's an easy way to cut into your budget. One thing to ask yourself is if you need to rent. Are you able to live with your parents or a family member for free or for a lot less than you would pay if you were renting? If so, you could potentially save enough money to purchase a house instead of renting.

It's important to think carefully about many factors of living, including whether to rent or buy. Let me start off by saying renting an apartment is perfectly okay to do. There are perks to renting, especially if it is for a short period of time. If you can split the rent with a roommate or multiple roommates, that is even better because it cuts down your cost. In renting a home or apartment, you'll generally be able to spend less time maintaining your place of living and this may allow you to get a part-time job or work to set up some passive income streams which will help you grow your wealth.

A Smart Guide to Building Wealth:
Money Moves Your Parents Wish They Had Made

If you can swing it, buying property or a home is better than renting. I know you may be thinking there's no way you can purchase a home. Yes, the initial down payment can be a large sum to save up, but let me break it down for you. A typical 30-year mortgage payment with a 4% interest rate for a home that is $100,000 is around $500 per month. Now that sounds like something much more affordable! Then take it one step further. What if you bought this house and had a roommate paying you rent of $300 a month? They are saving money because it's cheaper than an apartment, and you're earning even more money. I call that a win-win! Maybe they stay with you for only six months, but that still comes to $1,800 you didn't have before. Now with a saving mentality, you can take that $1,800 and put it towards any debt you have.

Below is an example of how you could afford a $200,000 home. Your mortgage is slightly more, but with even one renter, you are cutting your mortgage in half. With two renters, you are now earning a profit. Do not purchase a home having to rely on rental income to pay for it, but do know it could be a better option instead of continuously renting from someone else in the future.

Mortgage & Rent Scenario

Months	Mortgage Cost	Rental Revenue 1 Renter	Rental Revenue 2 Renters	2 Rental Revenues - Mortgage
1	$1,000	$600	$1,200	+$200
6	$6,000	$3,600	$7,200	+$1,200
12	$12,000	$7,200	$14,400	+$2,400
18	$18,000	$10,800	$21,600	+$3,600
24	$24,000	$14,400	$28,800	+$4,800

When it comes to buying a home, you may not realize you have a few different options. Maybe purchasing your first home is way too expensive in the area where you live, and you feel like your only option is to rent something. There are other housing options you can purchase, including a townhome or condo. These can be great alternatives and may even be less expensive than your typical detached home. The one extra fee with these options might be a homeowners' association (HOA) fee. An HOA fee is typically an extra cost for the association to maintain the property and common living spaces. An HOA fee might cover landscaping, snow removal, garbage pickup, community pool maintenance, etc. Oftentimes, these fees are not large monthly costs, but be sure to check that you aren't getting into any astronomical fees on top of your mortgage payment.

The biggest reason buying is more advantageous than renting a home is because you will be building equity. Home equity is equal to the difference between the current market value of the home and how much you owe. For example, if the home is worth $100,000 and you still owe $75,000, your equity in the home is equal to $25,000. The equity you have can now be used moving forward. Unlike when you are renting an apartment, the money you pay for the rental is toast. You are not investing your money into anything. You are simply paying for a place to live.

With home equity, it is a better investment of your money because you can use it again in the future and build upon it. Now that you have $25,000 in equity and want to sell your house for $100,000, you can take that $25,000 and use it when you purchase your next home. You don't have to start from ground zero because you have already invested $25,000. However, as a side note, when you sell your home there are realtor fees and other fees which you'll be responsible for, so you will probably have quite a bit less than the original $25,000.

Another benefit of owning a home is that you can reap the benefits of your home appreciating in value. Home appreciation is when the value of your home goes up based on the housing market and trends. If the housing market is positive, your home will continue to go up in value. After living in your home for three to five years, you may be able to sell your home for more money than what you originally bought it for.

So now that you have come around to the thought of being able to purchase a home, where should you start? Well, one thing you should know is that you should probably plan to live there for at least three to five years. The reason for this is because you don't want to lose money. You want to use the home as an investment and get out what you put into it when you decide to sell it. Typically, the housing market does not have huge surges in growth over one or two years. Therefore, you will need to be there about three years so that when you sell your home for $110,000, and you bought it for $100,000, you will not lose money. Again, realtor fees can be around 6-8%, so you won't be making a huge profit if you are only there a few years and aren't able to sell your home for more than what you purchased it for.

If you decide to stay in your home for a few years, there are a couple ways to get more out of your investment. Yes, you have a 30-year loan, but does that mean you can't pay it off sooner? The short answer is no. One easy trick is to pay a couple hundred dollars more than what your mortgage is for each month. If the minimum payment each month is $500, then pay

$700 or $800 if you can. Over time, you will knock down that home loan by adding a little bit of an additional amount. Not to mention, you will also have more equity.

30-Year Mortgage for $180,000 House

Year	Paying Minimum Balance	Paying $200 More
1	$6,000	$8,400
10	$60,000	$84,000
15	$90,000	$126,000
20	$120,000	$168,000
21.4	$128,400	$180,000
30	$180,000	
		Saved almost 9 years!

Another trick that can help your home investment is to look into refinancing your home when interest rates are lower. Let's say you originally bought your home at a 4% interest rate, but now the market is down to a 2% interest rate. This might be a time to refinance your existing home loan.

Refinancing is when the bank allows you to get the current interest rate on your loan that is better than your original purchase interest rate. In the long run, this could help reduce your overall cost. All you have to do is go back to your bank or shop around to another bank and see if they would help you refinance at a lower rate. A lower rate equals more money in your pocket over time, because you now owe the bank less on your home. Sometimes the fees to refinance may be too expensive, so make sure you shop around to get the best deal to determine if it's worth doing.

Real estate can be a great avenue where you can get into building passive income. Passive income is just that—money that is coming in without doing anything. The work has already been set up on the front end, and now you get to reap the rewards. A simple example of this is rent. Let's say you have some money to invest into a duplex or to purchase a home with multiple rooms you can rent out. Each month, you will have a mortgage payment to pay on the home you bought—let's say $1,500. However, you now have renters who will be paying you each month. For each room, you are charging $500 including utilities. With four rooms being rented you are now bringing in $2,000, which is $500 more than you owe on your mortgage. You are now earning extra money each month through this investment. Over time, that extra income will grow into what could be a large sum of money. If you continue to invest in more properties, this could multiply very quickly.

Rental Income

Months	Income (Rent x 4 People)	Expenses (Mortgage)	Total Revenue
1	$2,000	$1,500	$500
12	$24,000	$18,000	$6,000
24	$48,000	$36,000	$12,000

Rent is just one example of passive income. Creating passive income streams can be a lot of work to set up, but can be very vital in creating more wealth for you in the long run. Just think if you were able to make money while you sleep. Count me in!

Passive income can come in many forms. One simple way is to create something of value that you can continuously sell. Maybe you created an app, wrote a book, or designed a digital file, such as a poster, to sell. You only have to create it once and then you can sell it to as many people as you can over and over again. You could also look at renting out your home or your car when it's not in use for cash. Again, still takes a little work, but is an easy way to have cash flowing in without a lot of effort.

Recently, social media has been an avenue to provide passive income. Having a large following on social media platforms, subscribers to a YouTube channel, a popular podcast, or being a competitive gamer could end up in collecting a ton of money. If you have a large following, you may get brands reaching out to you to promote their products and paying you to do so. You can also cash in for every click or every ad that is watched on your channel or site. Once you develop and provide the content, it can live on forever and be monetized each time. Not everyone is going to be successful, but if you can find a niche that is relevant to a lot of people, it may be worth sharing your content and insights for money in the long run.

There are many ways to create passive income streams, which can become more complex than the examples above. As you get going with your financials, you can start looking into investing into other passive income options like dividend-paying stocks, credit card cashback rewards, peer-to-peer lending or investing into a high yield savings account or CD. If you do some research, there are lots of possibilities that might fit what is best for you. Again, the great thing about setting up passive income is that it is continuously providing you with an income stream without much effort once it's up and running. This could be very important in the future if you were to lose a job or could even supplement you with additional income if you had a large expense come up.

Chapter 7: Investments

Don't be intimidated by the word investing. Once you have understanding, there is nothing to fear. You are putting your money somewhere it can grow quicker rather than letting it sit in the bank not earning much over time. Free money, I'll take it! When it comes to investing your money into different options, there are multiple ways to do it. There are also many different paths that can work. The only key is to get rid of any bad debt first before you start moving into any type of investing.

Everyone thinks retiring is just something you do. That's not the case. You have to work hard and save money *now* in order to retire with enough money to cover your bills. Otherwise, you may be forced to work until much later in life than you would prefer or could physically handle. The first chance I had to understand retirement and how to get started saving money was when I was working in my first job at a corporation.

Getting a job with benefits is where you may encounter a 401(k). With most employers, you are given a salary, and you can also contribute into a 401(k), also known as a retirement fund. Typically, big corporations offer a contribution match into your retirement fund after you have been an employee for a certain amount of time. If you choose to start saving 3% of your salary into your 401(k), your employer may match your investment at a certain percentage. If you give 5% and they choose to match 3%, that is essentially free money coming from them. Like I have said before, free money is the best money! Now, if they are willing to match 5%, for example, then why wouldn't you put in at least 5%? You are missing out on free money! So always put in at least the amount your company is willing to match. Capitalize on those chances, because every opportunity can start to add up over time. Remember, with compounding interest, the more you save now, the more it will grow for you to retire with.

Employer Matching 5% of 401(k) Contributions

Year	Paying Only 3% Match	Paying Full 5% Match	Free Money Missed
1	$1,200	$2,000	$800
5	$6,000	$10,000	$4,000
10	$12,000	$20,000	$8,000

A Smart Guide to Building Wealth:
Money Moves Your Parents Wish They Had Made

When it comes to a 401(k), where exactly is your money going? Typically, your employer gives you the option to choose from a variety of mutual funds. They range from high risk to low risk. A mutual fund is a pool of money that is professionally managed and includes money from many investors and assets, including stocks and bonds. Yes, the stock market can fluctuate, but by investing in a variety of assets, your money will be safe in the long run.

The benefit of a mutual fund is that you are diversifying your risk because of the variety of assets you are investing in. As the saying goes, "Don't put all your eggs in one basket." Don't put all of your money in one asset. The reason for this is if that one asset fails, you are not completely broke. By putting your money into a pool of multiple assets, you are reducing that risk. Each mutual fund is constantly updating and managed so that the total amount of money grows over a long period of time.

If you are young you should be putting your money into in a high-risk mutual fund. Take into consideration your risk tolerance, but you potentially have at least 30 years ahead of you until retirement, so you don't need to access that money for a long time. High risk can equal high reward. Markets will always fluctuate in the short term, but over long periods of time, mutual funds typically have an upward trajectory. As you start getting closer and closer to retirement, you won't want any major shifts in your money because you will need to access it and live off of it. Therefore, you should slowly move to the low risk category of mutual funds as you get close to retiring.

With a 401(k) you may also hear the term vested interest. The amount of money that you contribute to your personal 401(k) is always vested interest. However, the amount your company will match you is not. Vested interest is when your employer's contribution to your retirement account is fully yours, even if you leave the company. Vested interest typically occurs when you have been at your company for a specific length of time—could be a year or much longer. It can pay off if you can stay at a company for a few years rather than jump from one company to another, especially when it comes to your retirement account—something to think about before quickly getting into a new job.

Once I had contributed to my 401(k), I started looking into more options to invest. I had a few thousand dollars sitting in my savings account that could either sit there or be put to good use. Every time I found I had a surplus in my savings account, I would try investing that money. At first, it was just $1,000 at a time. I knew that if it sat any longer in my savings account, I would find a way to spend it on something senseless rather than investing it. Out of sight is out of mind. I would not miss the money if it wasn't there.

I decided to look into a Roth IRA, which is investing into mutual funds that grow exponentially over time and is similar to your 401(k). Essentially, I use it as another type of savings account, but it's better. With a Roth IRA, you are putting money into an account and paying taxes on it now. Over the years, the money is growing tax FREE. Free is my favorite four-letter word! Yes, there is a catch. Because your money is growing tax free, you can only contribute a certain amount of money into this account each year. As of 2020, you could only contribute $6,000 for each person. If you have a spouse, you can contribute up to $12,000 total. Another catch is you can also only take out the amount you put in. If you put in $5,000, you can only get out $5,000. You cannot get out any of the extra earnings until you reach 59.5 years old, but you can always quickly access the money you put in there.

With my personal Roth IRA, I have found I am getting a year over year return of at least 10% or more on what I am putting in. That return rate is huge! A typical savings account you will only get a return of 2% or less. With a Roth IRA, I am making a much bigger return than if my money was sitting in normal bank account. This is the underlying theme of investing—where can I put my money so that I can earn a bigger return than if it just sat in a typical savings account?

My personal plan is to use my Roth IRA as my extra savings account or emergency fund if I need it. It's relatively quick to access my money and it's growing at a higher rate than a typical savings account over time. I am also planning to use a Roth IRA when it comes to saving up for my children's college instead of other education plans, such as a 529 plan. Those plans have stricter stipulations on how you can use that money and make it much tougher to get to your money if you need it.

Having a healthy body and mind is another way to invest in yourself and your wealth. Don't underestimate the wealth of good health. Medical expenses can be a huge hole of debt you can get into if you don't properly take care of what you put into your body and if you aren't moving it properly. If you don't take care of your body now, you may set yourself up to be sick later in life. Smoking is the perfect example of this. Yes, you can be healthy when you're young, choose to smoke, and have no issues at the time. However, years later if you are still smoking, you will have lasting effects such as cancer and potentially years taken from your life expectancy.

Staying active and healthy can help your body fight off illness and is also very beneficial for your mental health. One way I get around a gym expense is I have a makeshift gym in one of our spare bedrooms, complete with dumbbells, bands, and other equipment. If that isn't possible, there are reasonably priced gym memberships you can be a part of. Stay away from the gyms that have astronomical monthly fees, especially if you decide not to go regularly or won't use all of their offered services. When in doubt, you can always find plenty of free workout videos online or use an app where you don't need any gym equipment at all.

Another way to set yourself up for success in terms of your health and medical expenses is to set up a health savings account or HSA with your employer. An HSA is a savings account where you can allocate money that is pre-taxed to use only on qualified medical expenses. Basically, with an HSA, any money you decide to put in that account for the year can be rolled over automatically each year and used for the rest of your life on anything medical. There is no time limit on those funds. If you don't use it now, you can use it 10 or 20 years from now if you need to. That is why it is great!

You can build up your HSA for when you plan to have a family, an emergency surgery, or routine prescriptions. Chances are you will have routine doctor visits at the very least, which could still cost you. The important thing is that having money already on hand will help by not taking a huge cut into your monthly budget. You already have a backup. The only catch is not everyone can open an HSA. You must have health benefits through your employer and be on a specific benefits plan in order to have the option to open an HSA. If you have the option to open one, I highly recommend it.

Chapter 8: Other Ways to Save

There are other small tips and tricks that should not be overlooked because, over time, they start to really add up and help save a ton of money. One of the biggest budget breakers can be going out to eat too much. For one thing, I always take my lunch to work. It will be healthier than what I would get if I went out for food and it's much cheaper. An easy way to get in the habit is to make a lot of food for dinner the night before so you always have a tasty leftover meal to take with you the next day for lunch.

Do not waste your money buying lunch or coffee every single day. That is money you are throwing down the drain. If you want coffee, fine. Make a delicious, inexpensive one at home or a free one at work. Why do you need to spend $25 or more a week going to the coffee shop? That's the price of a delicious meal at a nice restaurant.

Small purchases add up over time. Choose experiences over things. Just think, instead of a coffee every day for a month, maybe you can afford a plane ticket to New York City!

Experiences are much more meaningful than material items any day. Find ways to make your money go as far as possible. Don't get me wrong, going out to eat and trying new restaurants is one of my favorite things to do, but do it wisely. Aside from special occasions, going out to eat should be done sparingly.

Typically, for me, I allocate to go out to dinner once a week. I want the meal to be special and worth my money. On the weekends, it's a nice treat to not make dinner for a night. However, going out to eat every night can cut into your budget in a big way. A couple of tips if you do decide to go out to eat include not getting an appetizer, as well as limiting alcohol. Alcohol is the one thing that can make your bill skyrocket. If possible, drink something at home either before or after dinner as a way to save a few bucks. Plus, water is FREE!

Earlier, I talked about how shopping can personally become a bit of a weak spot if I let it. There are always new trends to try for clothes, hair, and beauty, which is why it's difficult for me. My advice when it comes to shopping is to never pay full price. There are many ways to get around this. If you are shopping for clothes, can you find a promo code online to save money or get free shipping? Can you use your credit card rewards points towards a large purchase? Can you watch and wait for your item to go on sale next week? Sales are constantly happening, so just be sure to time it right. Or put the item in your cart and wait a few days until they send you an email with a code to save on those items.

Are you wanting to buy pricier items, like furniture or electronics? Items like these go on huge discounts around big holidays, like Black Friday or Labor Day. Figure out what you want and then wait to purchase it for much less during those holiday sale periods for 50% off or more. And remember, just because something is on SALE or marked FREE does not mean you need it or will even use it.

One way to consciously determine your purchase is by thinking of how many hours of work it would take to afford that item. Chances are you don't need it that badly. Another creative way to save is to purchase something secondhand and turn it into what you want. I recently wanted a white dresser, so I found a gently used one on Facebook Marketplace, sanded it down, painted it white, and added new handles. It looked as good as new! That was such an easy way to save hundreds of dollars to get exactly what I wanted. There are many nice secondhand pieces you can find online, at garage sales, or in retail stores to refurbish into very nice items.

An easy way to save with your favorite retailers is to sign up as a loyalty member or get their app. If you frequently shop there, you may be able to earn points, get discounts, or even get the tenth burrito free! You can find tons of ways to save if you do a little extra research before you buy.

When it comes to hair, do you really need a new haircut every six weeks? Maybe not. You also don't need to color your hair or get your nails done frequently if you are trying to save. My advice is to stick to special occasions only if you really want an update. Hair and nail care can easily turn into thousands of dollars spent a year, which is the price of a mortgage payment on a house! Put things into perspective on where you want your money to go and what your big picture goals are.

Subscriptions can turn into another big expense of your budget. Check to see how many subscriptions you currently have. Do you really need them all? If you want and frequently use a TV subscription, that is fine, but do you need five? Most likely not. Can you share the subscription with someone to cut some costs? Try to eliminate subscription-based products as much as possible because those payments keep going with no end in sight. They reel you in, get your payment information, and charge it monthly whether you use it or not. Check which ones you really need to keep.

Let's look at another example. When it comes to music, do you really need ad free music for $10 a month or more than $100 a year? No, that is not a need. That is a quick way to reduce your expenses. Free music with a few more ads will work just as good and save you a boatload of cash.

Do you actually go to the gym? If not, get rid of that gym membership. Maybe you can find an online program or free app that will suffice for your exercise needs. Check to see what other subscriptions you have that may also be wasting some hard-earned money. These may include, but are not limited to, pet toy boxes, wine club boxes, makeup sample boxes, new clothes boxes, or meal delivery kits. It is one thing if you truly use these subscriptions and find it as a need, but it's another thing if you don't. This is a great way to cut out a bunch of expenses you can use towards better investments.

Most importantly, if you are trying to find small ways that add up to big savings, you need to hustle. Can you add more income quickly by picking up extra shifts or working overtime? Those hours add up and can produce a sizeable amount of money. Can you live at home with your parents to save on rent for a short time? Can you take public transit instead of leasing or buying a car? Can you sacrifice a couple months of not going out to eat so you can save up and pay down the rest of your debt? Small sacrifices and finding ways to hustle will pay off in a big way.

You won't grow your wealth by sitting around and letting the world pass you by. Yes, you will see other people throwing their money around and going out to eat for lunch and dinner every day, but you have goals that are much bigger than them. Make a small goal and then move on to your next. Take power of your wealth and help it grow. Save early and often because the more you do when you are young, the more it will pay off. Hustle now to enjoy later. Your wealth will be there waiting when you do!

Chapter 9:
Ready, Set, Go!

By now you should have a basic understanding of what it will take to get your financials headed in the right direction. Save and be conscious of where you are spending. Start with a budget to lay out all of your expenditures and income in one place. This will tell you a lot about your current state and where you should begin to make changes.

Begin to make small goals and start tackling your debt. Bad debt will impact your future if it is not taken care of, so you want to handle that first. If bad debt is all taken care of and you have an emergency fund in place, you can now use your surplus of money to invest. Find ways to minimize your risk and maximize your investments. The fun begins!

Having time on your side as a young person is a huge advantage when it comes to investing. Start now and use this time to put your money into areas that will grow lasting financial rewards. Your initial investment could be into a retirement fund such as a 401(k), Roth IRA, or into a health savings account. You could also start earning rewards with a credit card or purchasing a home, where you can develop passive income from renters. Save as much as you can as early as you can. The key is to just start!

Making conscious decisions in the right direction will continue to compound good decisions over time. It's going to take a lot of work but knowing *why* you are saving and having a purpose for each dollar you save or invest will make it easier to keep going. As you start to see more dollar signs, it will make it that much sweeter! Save now, for a rich future ahead of you.

www.ingramcontent.com/pod-product-compliance
Lightning Source LLC
Chambersburg PA
CBHW072033230526
45466CB00020B/1908